ALL I REALLY NEED TO KNOW I LEARNED FROM THE

Printed in the United States of America

First Edition

10 9 8 7 6 5 4 3 2 1

Library of Congress Catalog Card Number: 01-110831

ISBN: 0-7868-5333-6

Visit www.disneyeditions.com

ALL I REALLY NEED TO KNOW I LEARNED FROM THE

by Michael Mullin

If you can't laugh at yourself,
forget it.

Mickey's Birthday Party (1942)

Be larger than life.

Blue Rhythm (1931)

A job is a job,
no matter how odd.

Clock Cleaners (1937)

No adventure
is too big . . .

Alpine Climbers (1936)

. . . or too small.

The Little Whirlwind (1941)

Having a steady sweetheart
beats playing the field.

Puppy Love (1933)

**Optimism isn't just a way of life.
It's *the* way of life.**

Clock Cleaners (1937)

There are lots of ways
to be a hero . . .

Mickey's Fire Brigade (1935)

Touchdown Mickey (1932)

On Ice (1935)

Mickey's Christmas Carol (1983)

Clever beats buff . . .

Brave Little Tailor (1938)

. . . every time.

Brave Little Tailor (1938)

Question authority.

Steamboat Willie (1928)

Know a trick or two.

Magician Mickey (1937)

A little luck always helps.

Plane Crazy (1929)

**Fashion is fleeting.
Style is forever.**

Mickey's Gala Premiere (1933)

Be true to your friends, no matter
how hotheaded or simple they are.

Lonesome Ghosts (1937)

Big shoes mean good balance.

Mickey's Circus (1936)

A little mischief builds character.

Fantasia (1940)

Be the life of the party.

The Haunted House (1929)

Be a leader.

Fantasia (1940)

**Never let jealousy
get the best of you.**

Mickey's Rival (1936)

Get a dog . . . for life.

Society Dog Show (1939)

Remember special occasions,
and what makes them special.

Puppy Love (1933)

A kiss is worth
a thousand pictures.

Brave Little Tailor (1938)

Life is what you tailor-make of it.

Brave Little Tailor (1938)

Reward yourself sometimes.

The Prince and the Pauper (1990)

Upgrade to first class
whenever possible.

Clock Cleaners (1937)

Create a legacy that
makes people smile.

Steamboat Willie (1928)

Join a club.